TEA LOVER'S COLORING BOOK

Join our mailing list to be among
the first to find out about special offers,
discounts and our new releases!

Sign up at:
www.adultcoloringworld.net

ISBN-13: 978-1544628837
ISBN-10: 1544628838

@adultcoloringworld

facebook.com/adultcoloringworldbooks

@adultcolorworld

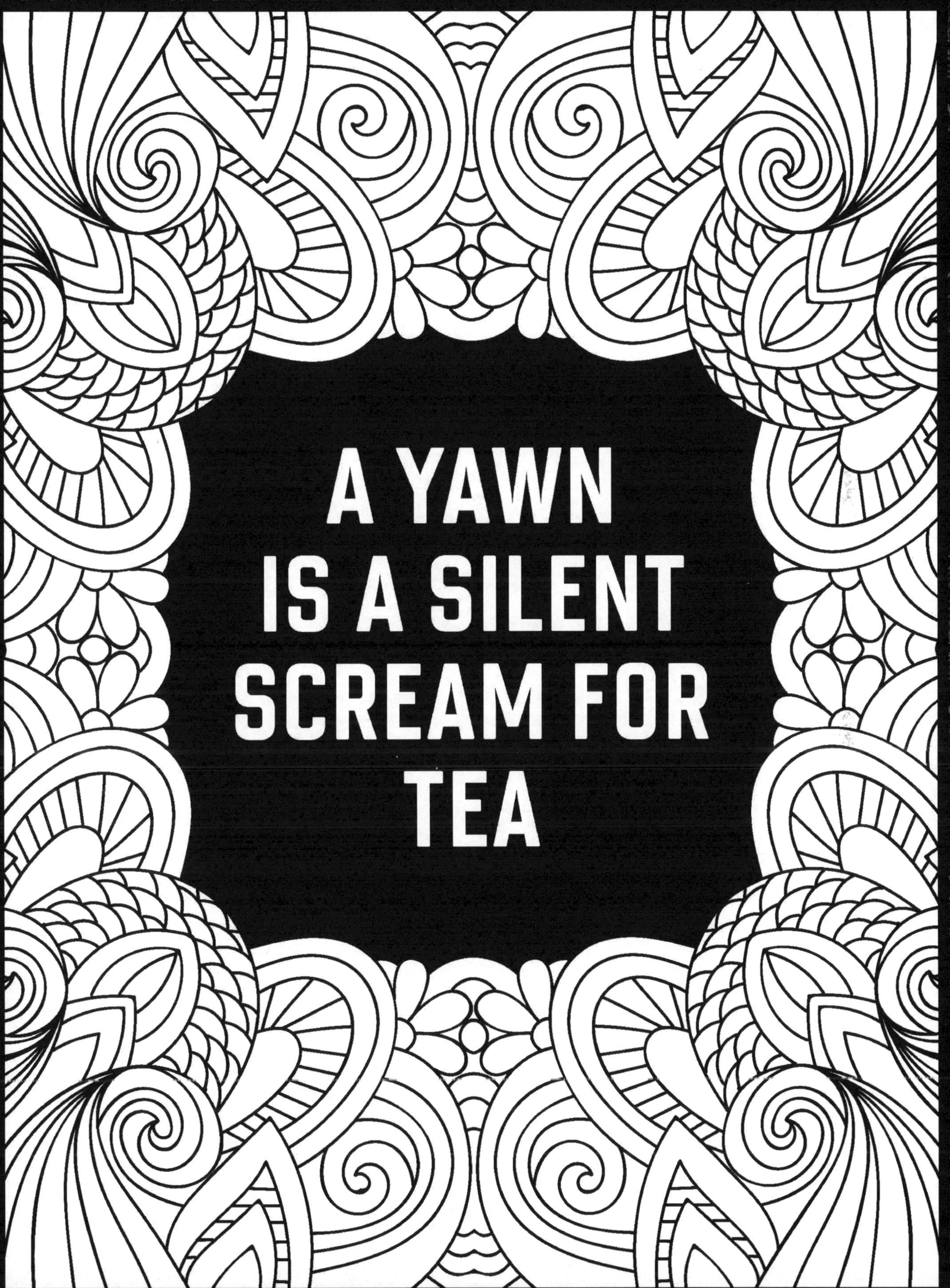
A YAWN
IS A SILENT
SCREAM FOR
TEA

CAN I CALL
YOU BACK IN
A FEW CUPS
OF TEA?

BE AMAZING TODAY
...BUT FIRST...
TEA

SOME DAYS
I MAKE TEA BUT
SOME DAYS TEA
MAKES ME

PROCAFFEINATING:
PUTTING THINGS OFF
UNTIL YOU'VE HAD
ENOUGH TEA

I ONLY
NEED TEA ON
DAYS ENDING
IN "Y"

MY FAVORITE
TEA? THE ONE WHERE
NO ONE TALKS TO ME
WHILE I DRINK IT

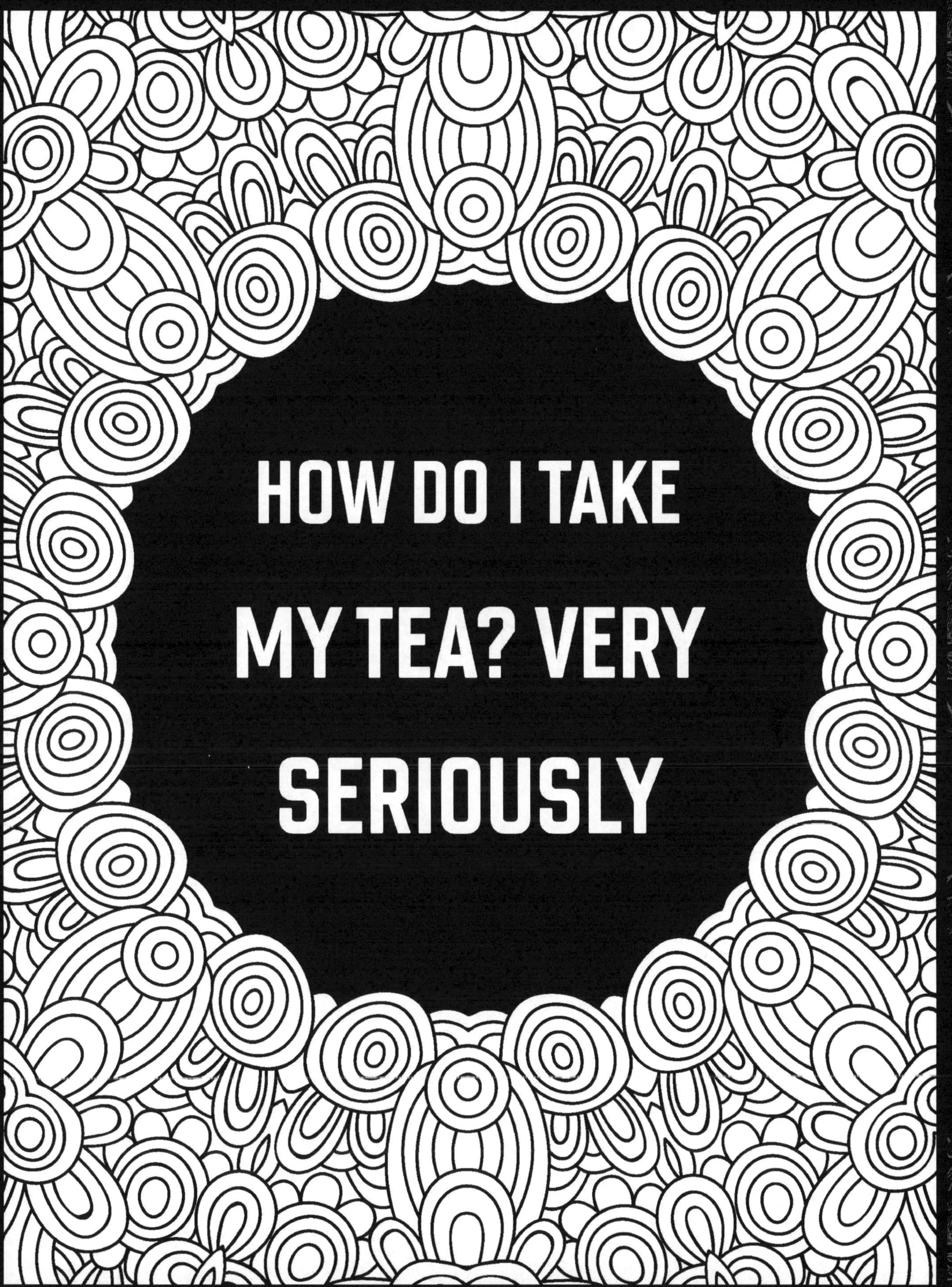
HOW DO I TAKE
MY TEA? VERY
SERIOUSLY

I MAKE
TEA DISAPPEAR
WHATS YOUR
SUPERPOWER?

LIFE IS TOO
SHORT TO DRINK
CHEAP TEA

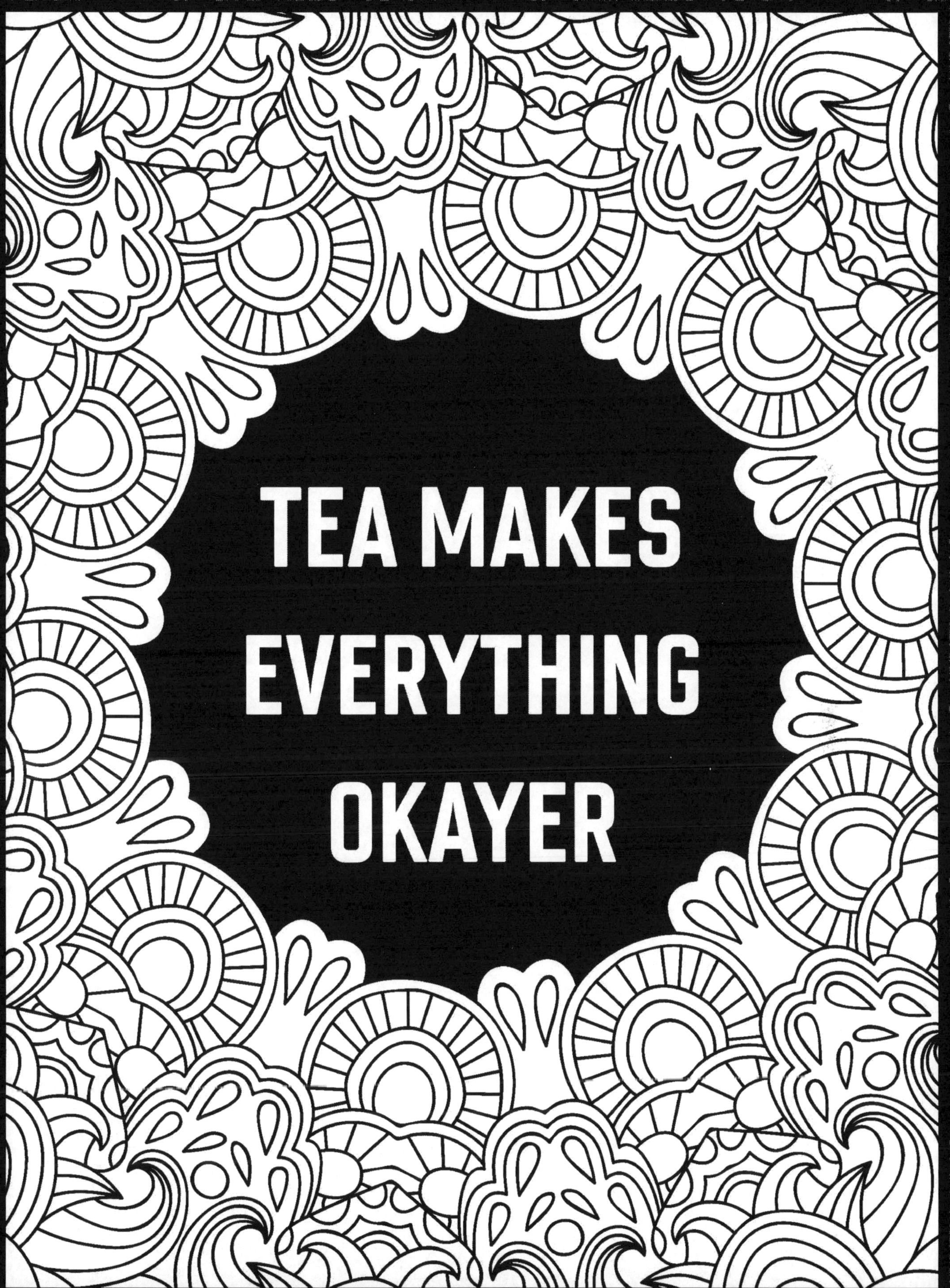
TEA MAKES
EVERYTHING
OKAYER

I'M ONLY
LIKE 103%
ADDICTED
TO TEA

LIFE
HAPPENS
TEA
HELPS

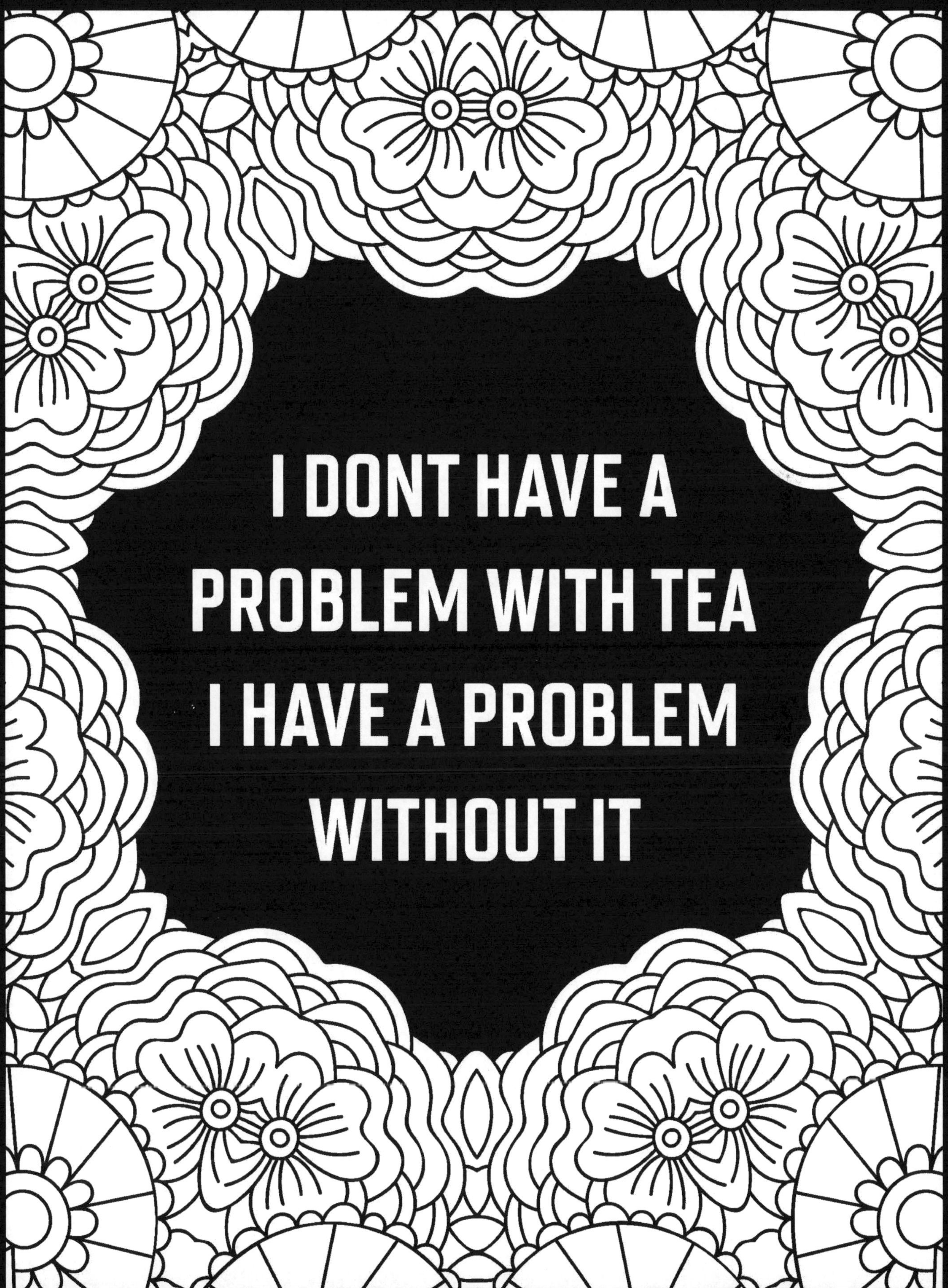
I DONT HAVE A
PROBLEM WITH TEA
I HAVE A PROBLEM
WITHOUT IT

HALF EMPTY
OR HALF FULL?
EITHER WAY IT'S NOT
ENOUGH TEA

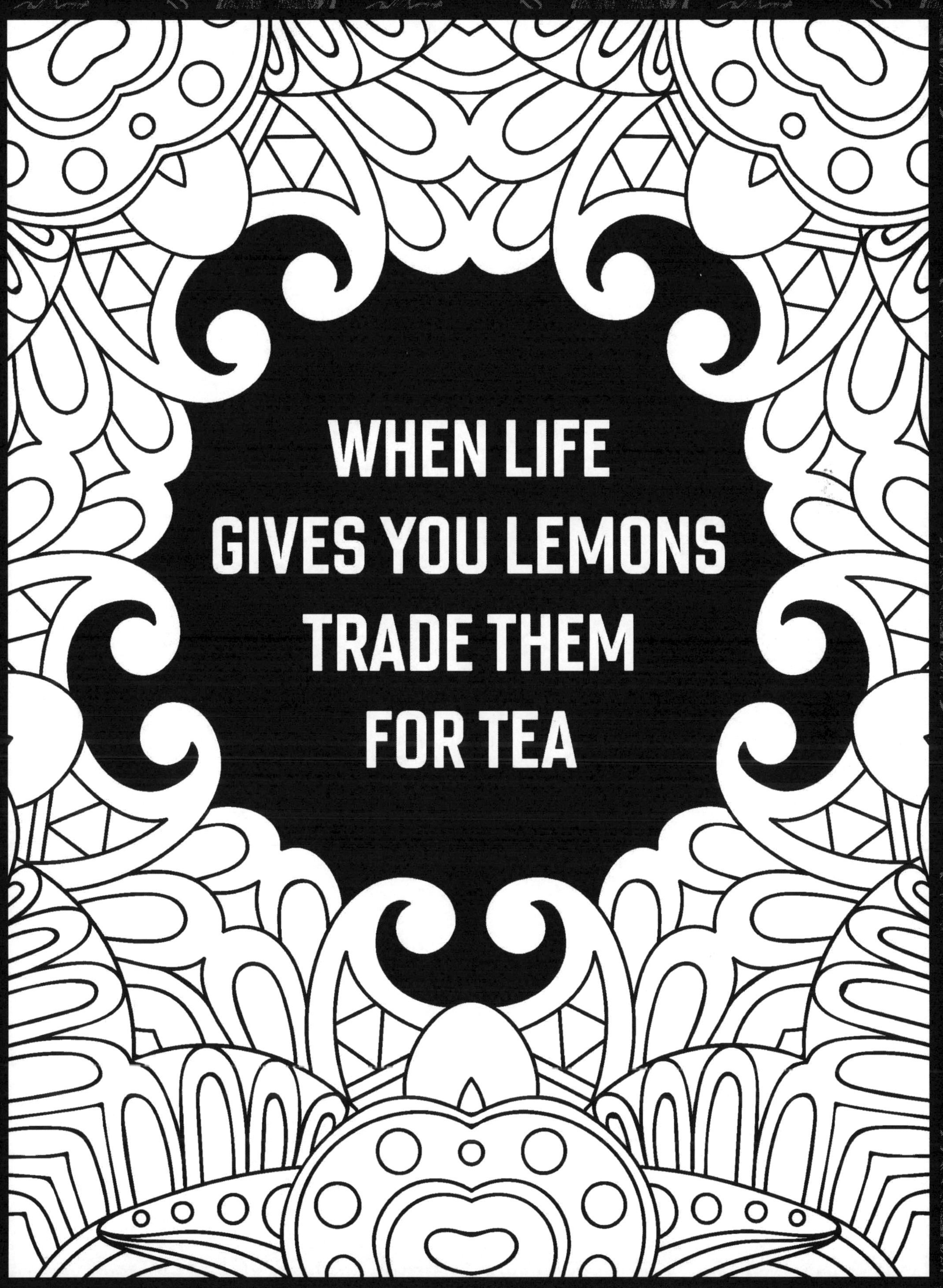
WHEN LIFE
GIVES YOU LEMONS
TRADE THEM
FOR TEA

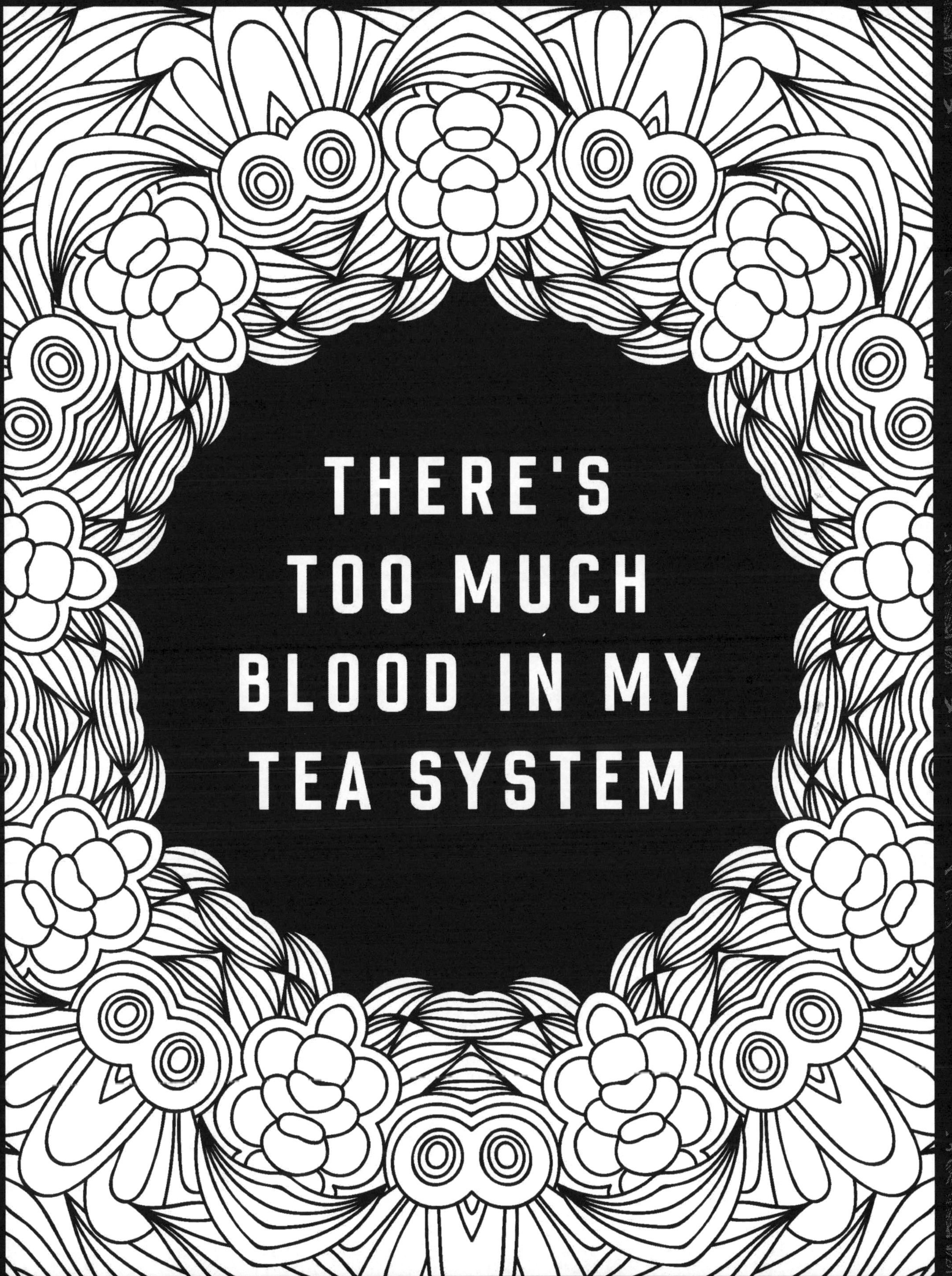
THERE'S
TOO MUCH
BLOOD IN MY
TEA SYSTEM

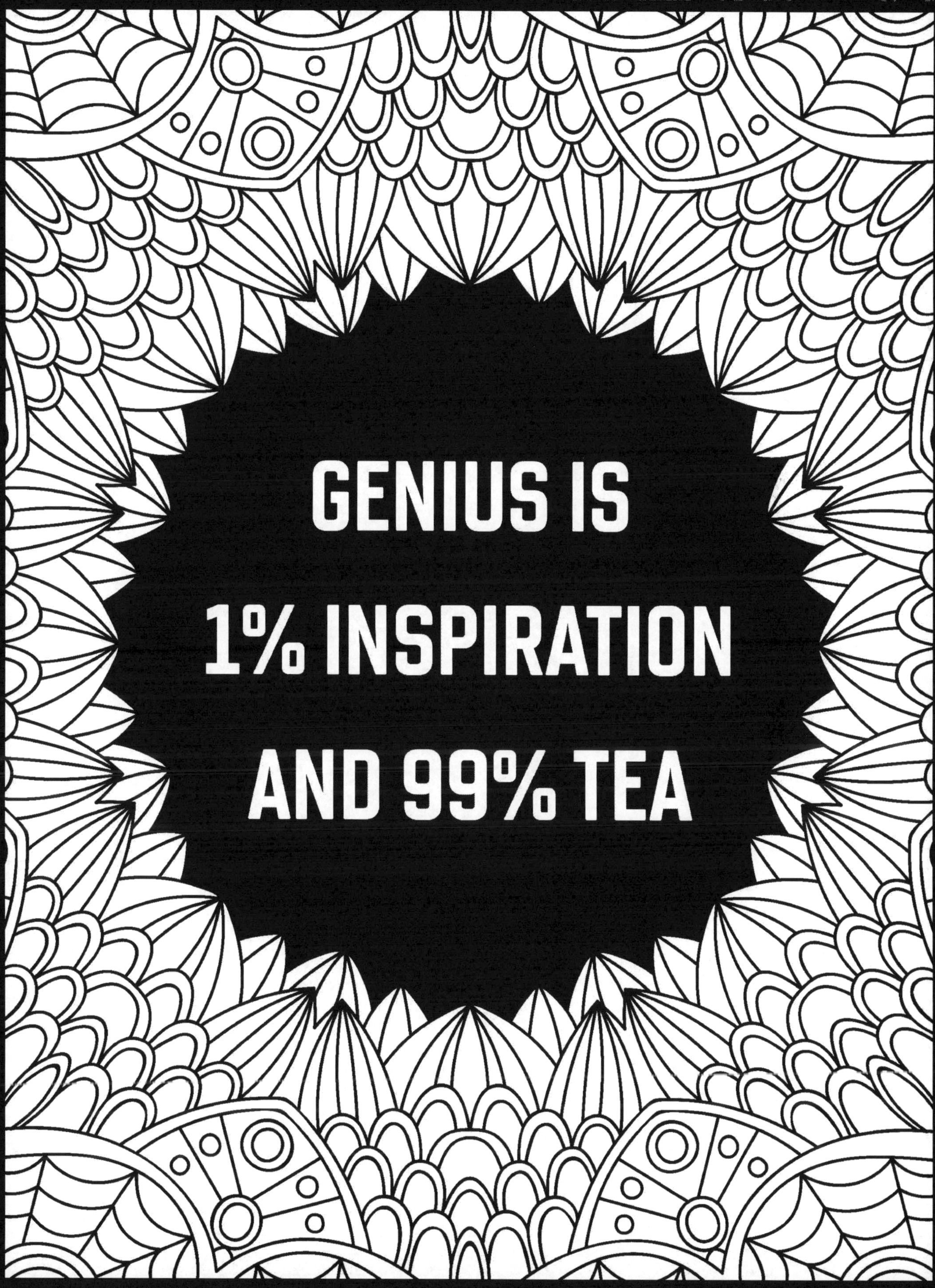
GENIUS IS
1% INSPIRATION
AND 99% TEA

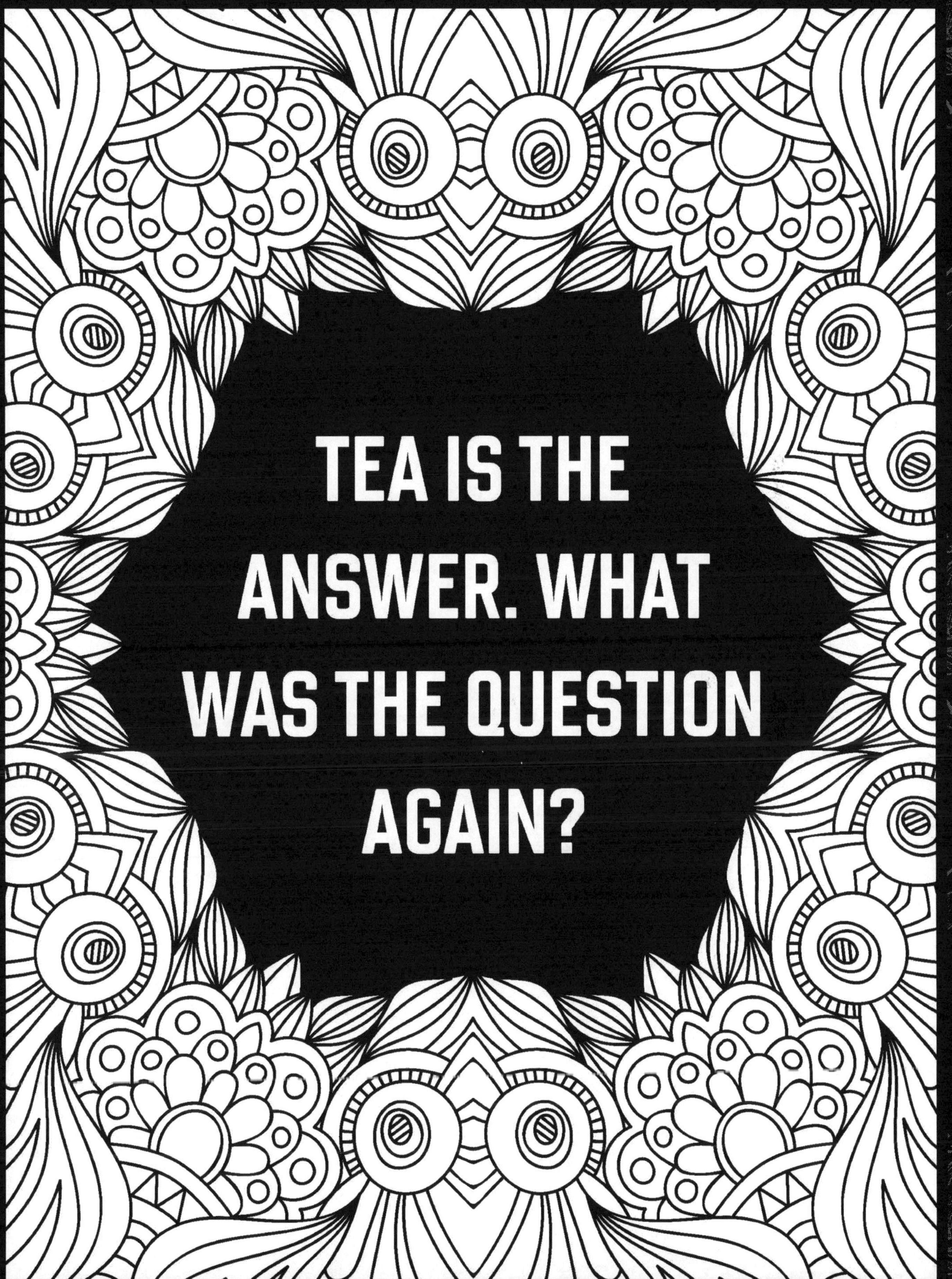
TEA IS THE
ANSWER. WHAT
WAS THE QUESTION
AGAIN?

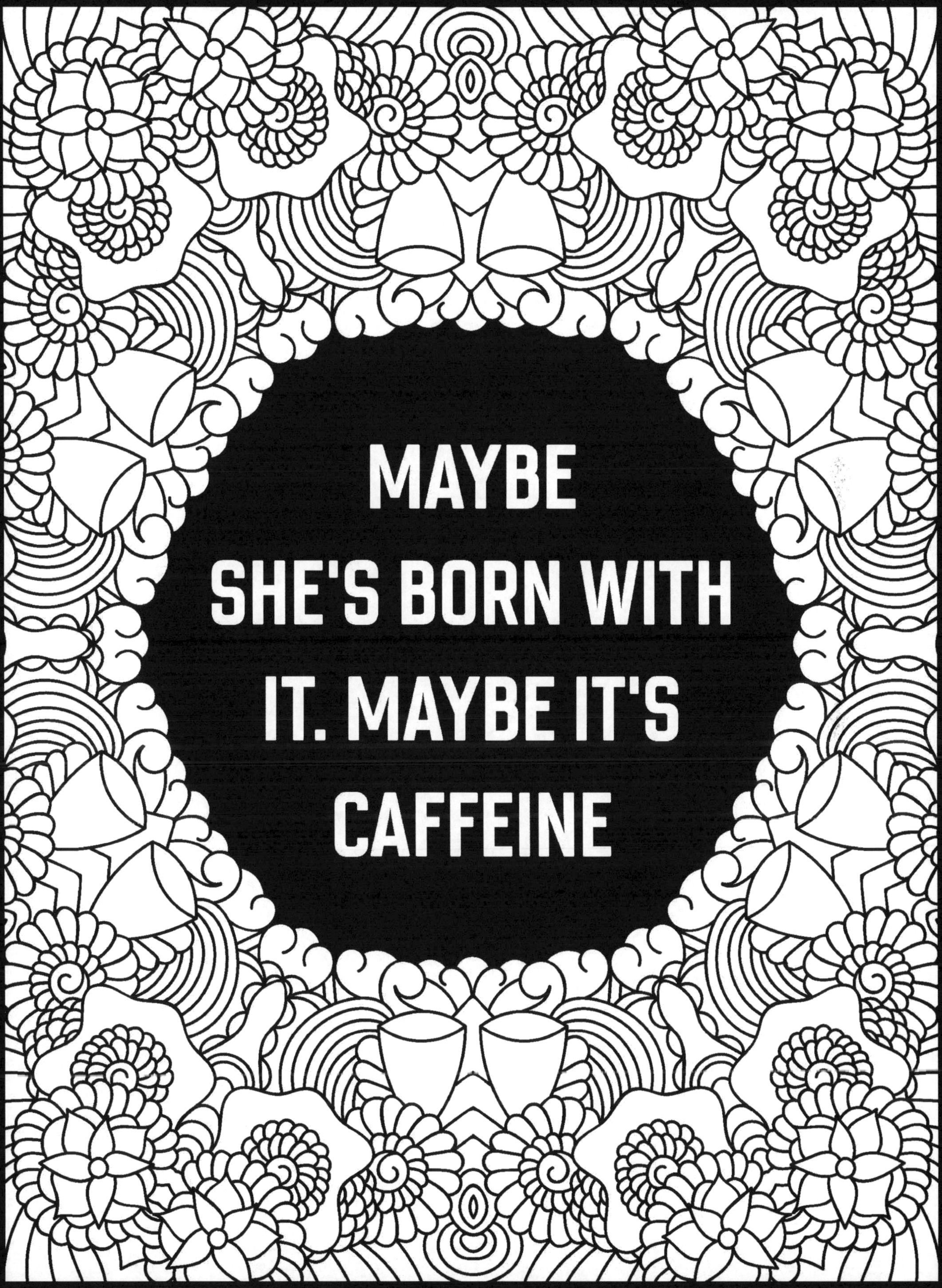
MAYBE
SHE'S BORN WITH
IT. MAYBE IT'S
CAFFEINE

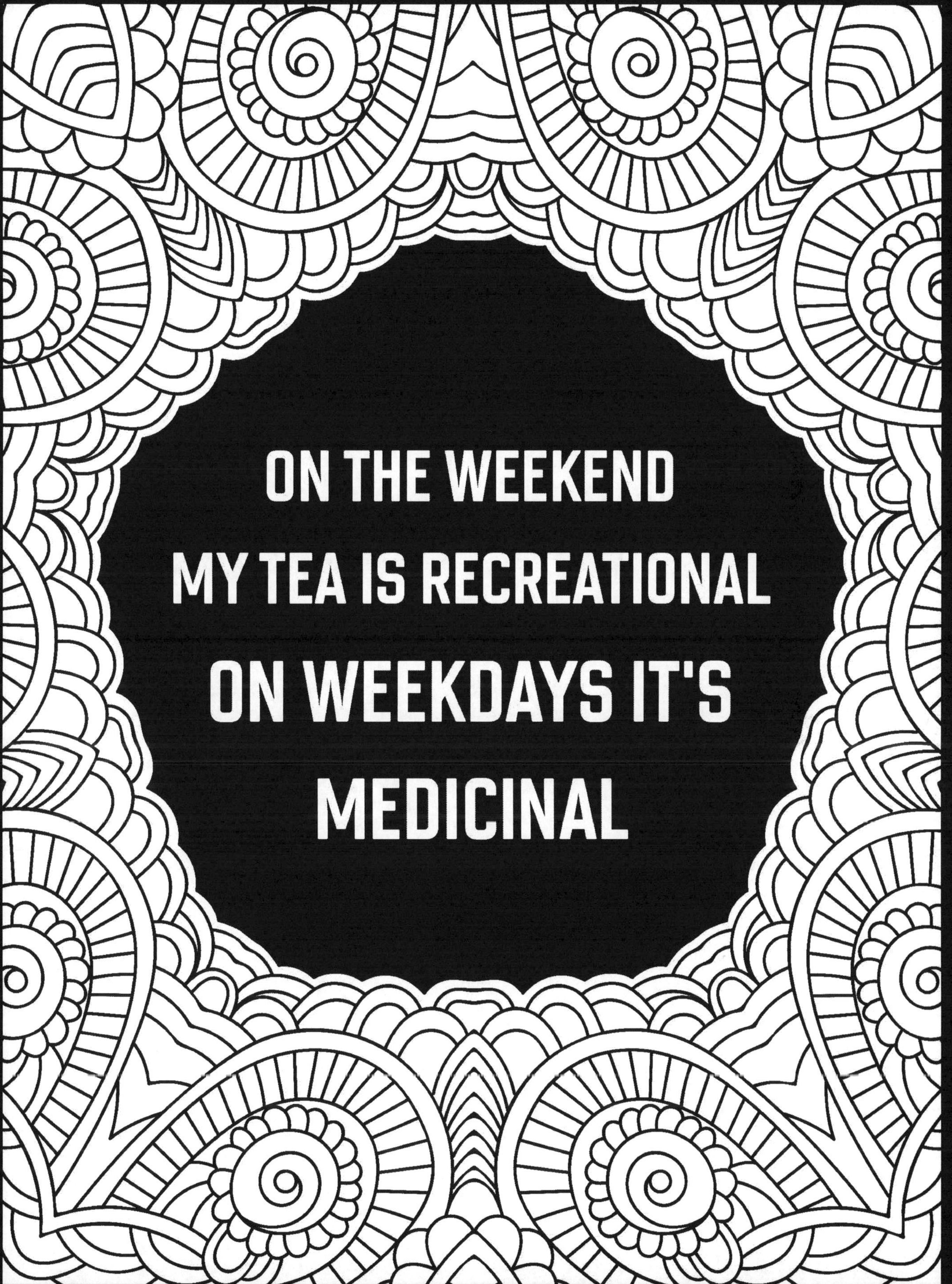
ON THE WEEKEND
MY TEA IS RECREATIONAL
ON WEEKDAYS IT'S
MEDICINAL

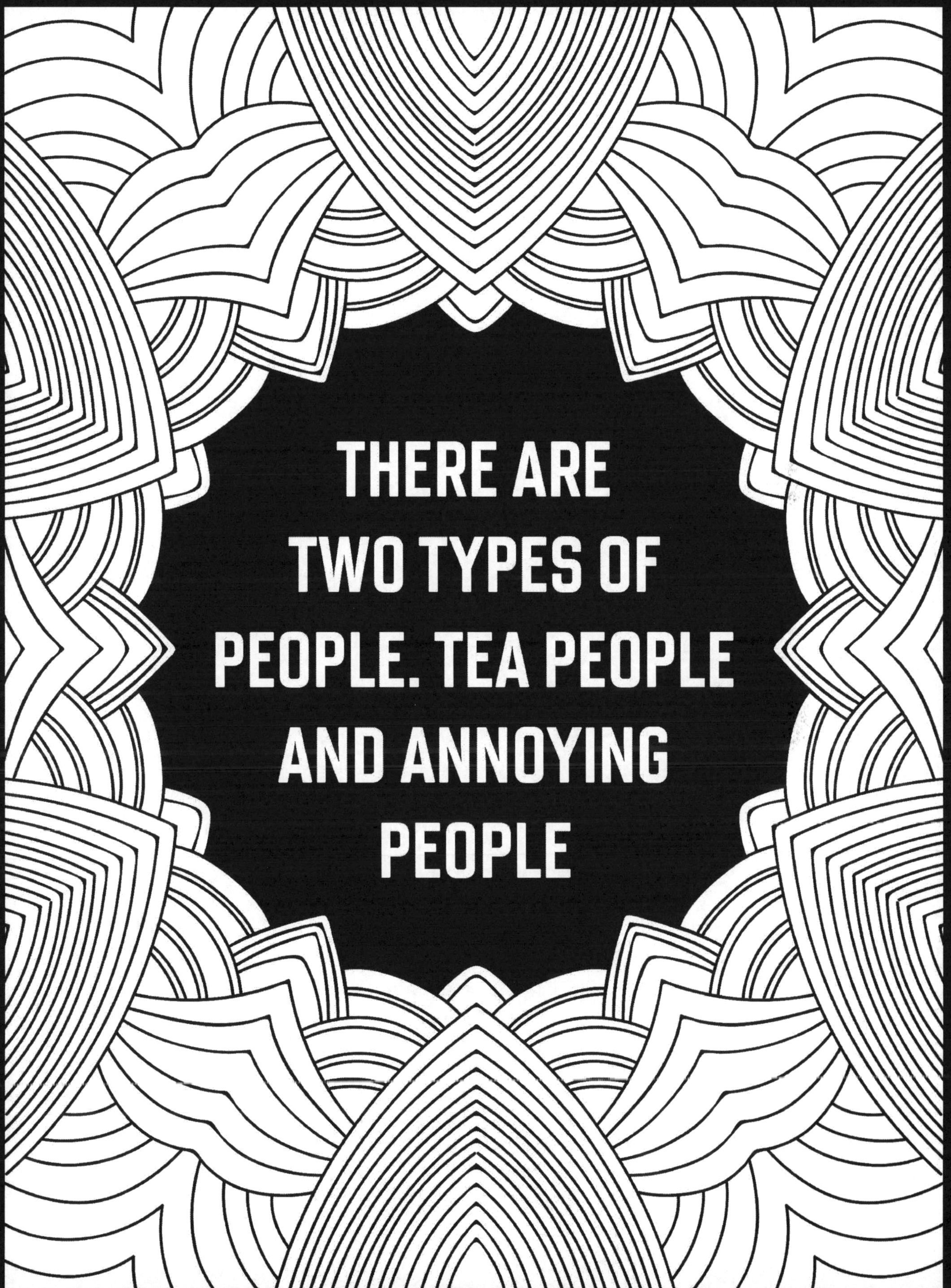
THERE ARE
TWO TYPES OF
PEOPLE. TEA PEOPLE
AND ANNOYING
PEOPLE

WAYS TO MY HEART:
BUY ME TEA
MAKE ME TEA
BE TEA

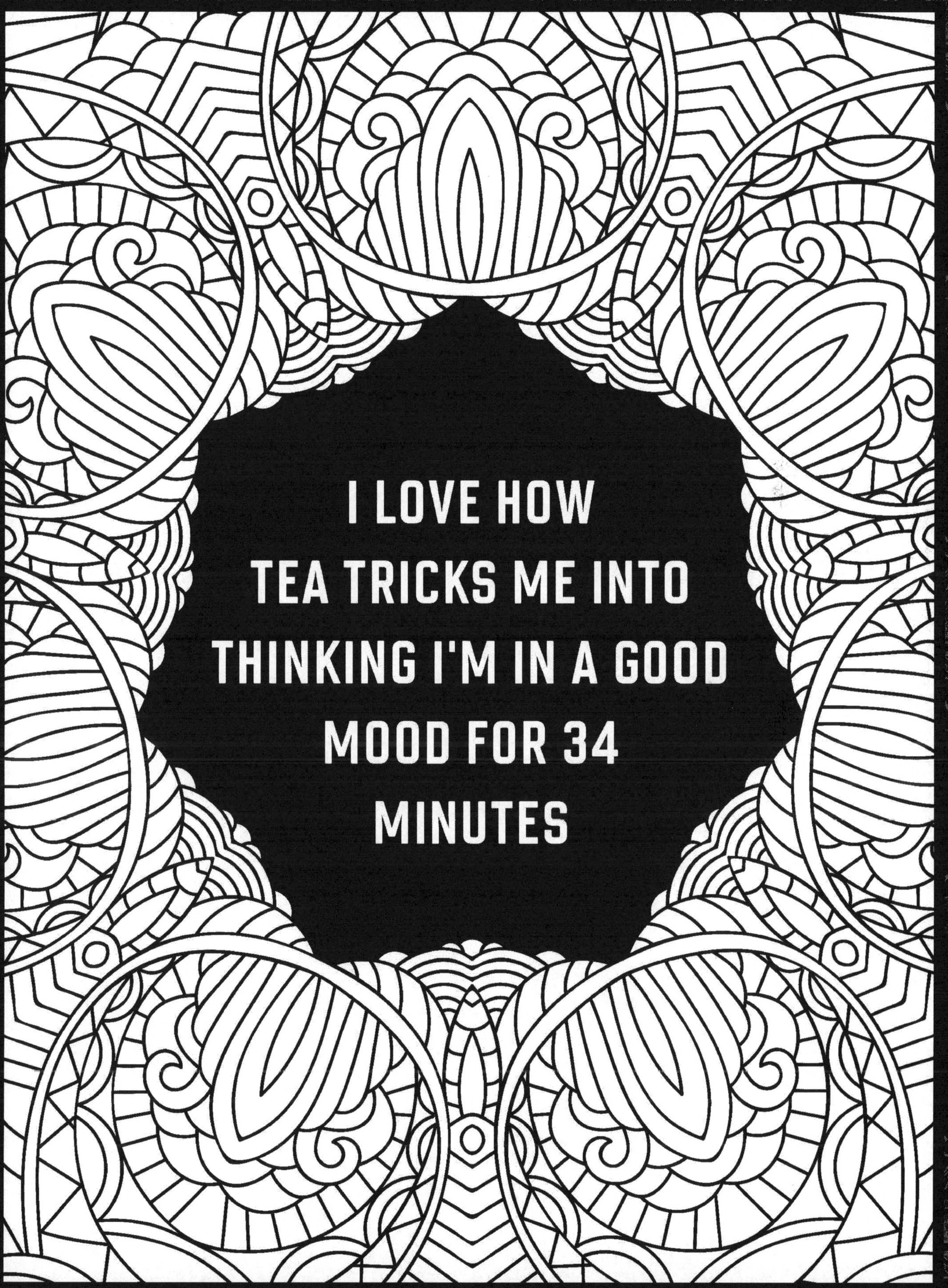
I LOVE HOW
TEA TRICKS ME INTO
THINKING I'M IN A GOOD
MOOD FOR 34
MINUTES

I'M NOT A TEA
ADDICT I'M JUST
EXCEPTIONALLY
CAFFEINE
ABSORBENT

NEVER
TRUST ANYONE
WHO DOESN'T
DRINK TEA

DOES SIZE
MATTER? IT DOES
IF YOU'RE TALKING
ABOUT THE SIZE OF
MY TEA CUPS

EVER FEEL
LIKE YOU'VE HAD
TOO MUCH TEA?
ME NEITHER

LET'S
GET THIS
PAR-TEA
STARTED

BLOOD
SWEAT
AND TEA

HIT ME
WITH YOUR
BEST POT

YOU CAN'T
BUY HAPPINESS
BUT YOU CAN
BUY TEA

TEA IS
CHEAPER THAN
THERAPY

FIGHT
FOR YOUR
RIGHT TO
POUR TEA

HELLO IS
IT TEA YOUR
LOOKING
FOR?

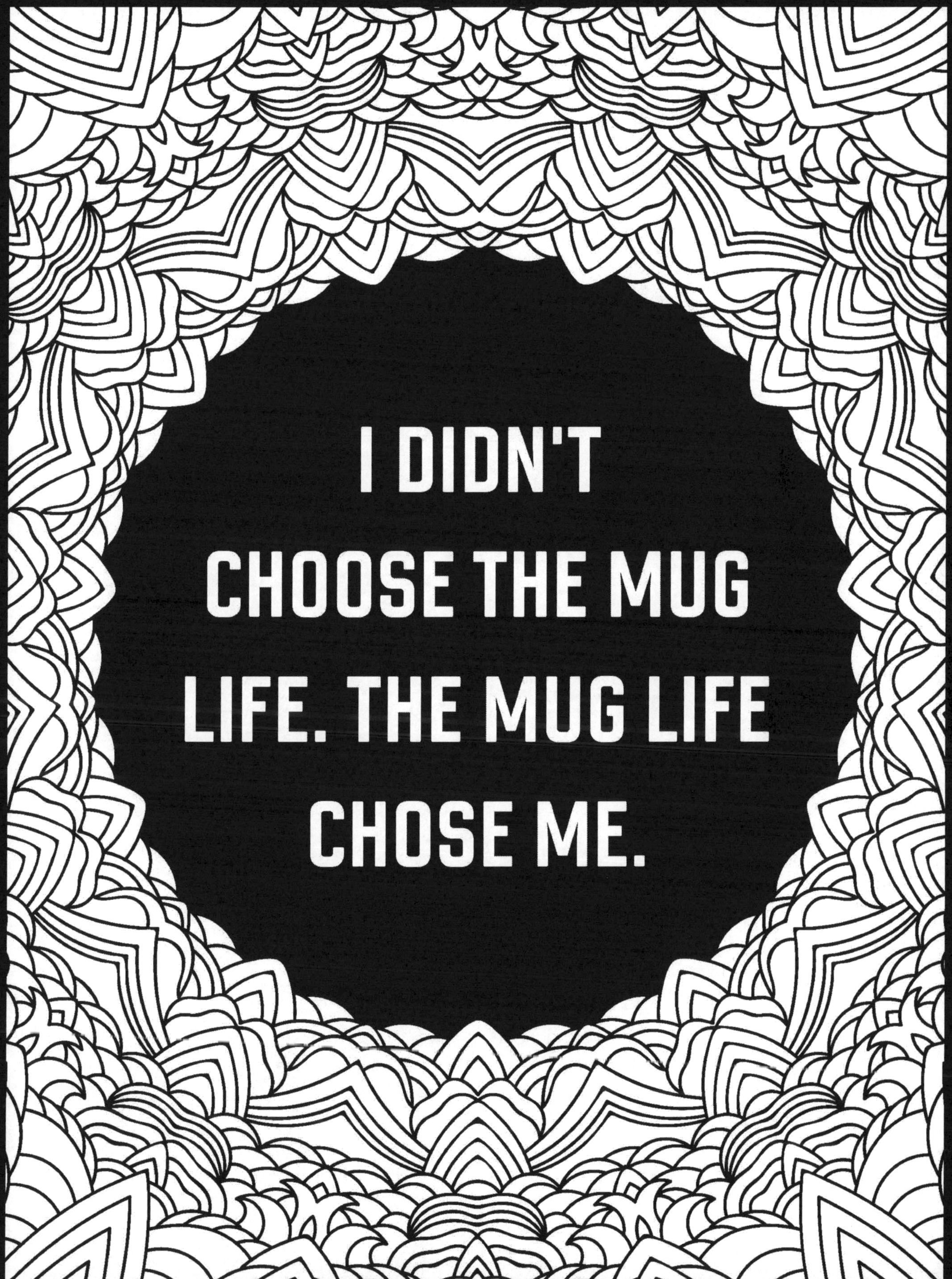
I DIDN'T
CHOOSE THE MUG
LIFE. THE MUG LIFE
CHOSE ME.

YOU ME
AND A CUP
OF TEA

NO ONE IS
EVERYONE'S
CUP OF TEA

THE BEST
TIME OF DAY
IS TEA:30

COLOR TEST PAGE

COLOR TEST PAGE

COLOR TEST PAGE

WE HOPE YOU
ENJOYED THIS BOOK!

TO VIEW OUR HUGE
RANGE OF ADULT COLORING
BOOKS, VISIT OUR WEBSITE
TODAY AND DON'T FORGET
TO FOLLOW US VIA OUR
SOCIAL ACCOUNTS!

25951451R00051

Made in the USA
San Bernardino, CA
14 February 2019